IMAGES OF WAR

FALLSCHIRMJÄGER: GERMAN PARATROOPERS 1942–1945

IMAGES OF WAR

FALLSCHIRMJÄGER: GERMAN PARATROOPERS 1942–1945

RARE PHOTOGRAPHS FROM WARTIME ARCHIVES

FRANÇOIS COCHET

Pen & Sword
MILITARY

AN IMPRINT OF PEN & SWORD BOOKS LTD.
YORKSHIRE - PHILADELPHIA

Originally published in Belgium by Editions de Krijger as *Fallschirmjäger: Les Parachutistes Allemands (Tome 2: 1942-1945)*

First published in Great Britain in 2019 by
Pen & Sword Military
An imprint of
Pen & Sword Books Ltd
Yorkshire - Philadelphia

ISBN 978 1 52674 070 0

Typeset in 12/14.5 Gill Sans by Aura Technology and Software Services, India
Printed and bound in India by Replika Press Pvt Ltd.

Pen & Sword Books Ltd incorporates the Imprints of Pen & Sword Books Archaeology, Atlas, Aviation, Battleground, Discovery, Family History, History, Maritime, Military, Naval, Politics, Railways, Select, Transport, True Crime, Fiction, Frontline Books, Leo Cooper, Praetorian Press, Seaforth Publishing, Wharncliffe and White Owl.

For a complete list of Pen & Sword titles please contact

PEN & SWORD BOOKS LIMITED
47 Church Street, Barnsley, South Yorkshire, S70 2AS, England
E-mail: enquiries@pen-and-sword.co.uk
Website: www.pen-and-sword.co.uk

or
PEN AND SWORD BOOKS
1950 Lawrence Rd, Havertown, PA 19083, USA
E-mail: uspen-and-sword@casematepublishers.com
Website: www.penandswordbooks.com

Contents

Introduction.. 7

Mini Glossary 8

Chapter 1
1942: The USSR 11

Chapter 2
Reinforcements and Various Projects 21

Chapter 3
Kampfgruppe Burckhardt and Fallschirm-Brigade Ramcke 32

Chapter 4
Fallschirm-Brigade Ramcke 33

Chapter 5
The Fallschirmjäger in Tunisia 39

Chapter 6
Italy (1943) 46

Chapter 7
The Aegean Sea (1943) 64

Chapter 8
Fighting in the East (1943-44) 68

Chapter 9
Italy (1944) 74

Chapter 10
The Normandy Invasion (1944) 89

Chapter 11
The Netherlands and the Ardennes 104

Chapter 12
'Until the Bitter End' 112

Introduction

The bloody fighting of the German *Fallschirmjäger* (paratroopers) of the Second World War has inspired a variety of books due to the fact that, assimilated to elite troops, airborne units of the Third Reich were regularly engaged at the forefront of the fighting. Famous victories, including the raid on the Belgian fort of Eben-Emael in May 1940 and the battles for control of the big island of Crete just a year later, remained in the collective unconscious, granting the paratroopers a kind of aura (sometimes a little exaggerated) and building an excellent esprit de corps amongst the troops.

In any case, however, the 'great age' of the *Fallschirmtruppen* (parachute units) was to end in 1941. From 1942 until the end of the conflict, German paratroopers were most often deployed in a more 'classical' way, although some battles (like Cassino or Leros) allowed them to reconnect with their recent and glorious past.

Image Credits - The majority of photographs in this book are from the author's collection, as well as those of several other people: Bernd Bosshammer, Jean-Pierre Chantrain, Jean-Louis Roba and Peter Taghon. Documents also come from *Der Adler* magazine and from various contemporary books on the *Fallschirmjäger*. Thanks must go to all those who helped to make this book.

Mini Glossary

Anvil: code name for the Allied landing at Anzio.

Brandenburg: unit of German 'commandos'.

Eiche: German code name for the liberation of Mussolini.

Eisbär: German code name for the invasion of the Italian-held Dodecanese islands (Battle of Kos).

EK: Iron Cross (*Eiserne Kreuz*).

Enigma: German machine which sent encrypted messages.

Fallschirmjäger: German paratrooper.

Felix: German code name for the planned invasion of Gibralter.

Festung: fortress.

FJD: German paratroop division.

FJR: German paratroop regiment.

Frhr: *Freiherr* (German title of nobility).

GI: American soldier (Government Issue).

Heer: German Army.

Hercules: German code name for the planned invasion of Malta.

HJ or Hitlerjugend: Hitler Youth.

Kampfgruppe: combat group.

KB: war correspondent.

Kessel: cauldron (designating a circled area).

Kübelwagen: a light military vehicle (the German 'jeep').

Luftwaffe: German Air Force.

Merkur: German code name for the invasion of Crete in May 1941.

Oberbefehlshaber: commander in chief.

Oberst: colonel.

Overlord: code name for the Allied landings in Normandy.

Panzerarmee Afrika (Panzer Army Africa): armoured African unit combining forces from *Afrika Korps* and Italian units.

Ritterkreuz: Knight's Cross of the Iron Cross.

Stösser: German code name for the final airborne operation in the Ardennes.

Sturmregiment: assault regiment.

Ultra: British military intelligence that decrypted the Enigma messages.

Wacht am Rhein: German code name for the final offensive in the Ardennes, December 1944.

Wehrmacht: collective name for the three branches of Germany's armed forces: *Heer* (Army), *Luftwaffe* (Air Force) and *Kriegsmarine* (Navy).

Useful dates for this volume

17 November 1941: German airborne assault on the River Neva.

2 December 1941: fighting on the Mus Front.

7 January 1942: arrival of *Kampfgruppe Burckhardt* in Africa.

21 March 1942: *KG Burckhardt* departs from Africa.

20 April 1942: paratrooper assault on the Volchov Front.

21 June 1942: fall of Tobruk.

19 August 1942: aborted Canadian landing at Dieppe.

23 October 1942: Allied offensive at El Alamein.

7 November 1942: the Ramcke Brigade succeeds in breaking the encirclement and regaining its lines.

8 November 1942: Allied invasion of North Africa.

13 May 1943: surrender of Axis forces in Tunisia.

10 July 1943: Operation Husky, the Allied landings in Sicily.

12 July 1943: paratroopers from 1. FJD arrive in Sicily as reinforcements.

26 July 1943: transfer of 2. FJD from France to Italy.

3 September: British troops invade Italian mainland.

8 September 1943: Italy surrenders.

9 September 1943: Allied landings at the Gulf of Salerno.

12 September 1943: Operation *Eiche*, the liberation of Benito Mussolini.

1 October 1943: fall of Foggia.

13 October 1943: Allied Army crosses the River Volturno.

12 November 1943: German paratroopers jump on Leros.

1 December 1943: Allied forces attack along the Liri Valley.

6 December 1943: 2. FJD in combat at Zhytomyr (present-day Ukraine).

22 January 1944: Allied landings at Anzio.

29 February 1944: 1. FJD relieves 90. Pz. Gr. Div. at Monte Cassino.

7 March 1944: 2.FJD retreats in Ukraine.

15 March 1944: Allied bombing of Monte Cassino and the destruction of the monastery.

10 May 1944: fighting on the Dnjerst.

18 May 1944: fall of Monte Cassino.

5 June 1944: fall of Rome.

6 June 1944: Allied landings begin in Normandy.

12 June 1944: 2. FJD retreats from the Eastern Front.

28 June 1944: German paratroopers fight in Lithuania.

20 July 1944: attempted assassination of the Führer.

25 July 1944: Operation Cobra (Allies) is launched in Normandy.

15 August 1944: Allied landings in Provence.

24 August 1944: liberation of Paris.

25 August 1944: start of the Battle for Brest, defended by men from Ramcke Brigade.

3 September 1944: fighting in the Mons Pocket.

20 September 1944: surrender of Brest.

17 September 1944: launch of Operation Market Garden.

21 September 1944: fall of Rimini.

17 October 1944: German paratroopers in action in East Prussia (Nemmersdorf).

16 December 1944: launch of *Wacht am Rhein*, the Battle of the Ardennes. failure of Operation *Stösser*.

28 February 1945: a battalion of *Fallschirmjäger* leave to reinforce Breslau Fortress.

20 March 1945: German paratroopers in action on the River Oder.

23 March 1945: the Allies cross the River Rhine (Operation Varsity)

14 April 1945: the Ruhr Pocket is cut in two by Allied forces.

19 April 1945: Allied forces reach the River Elbe.

8 May 1945: end of the Second World War in Europe.

Chapter 1

1942: The USSR

At the end of Volume I (*Fallschirmjäger: German Paratroopers 1937–1941*), we had left the German paratrooper in a very sad state by the end of 1941. The terrible losses suffered during the Battle of Crete (the 'tomb of the German paratrooper', in the words of General Kurt Student) were going to be very difficult to fill.

The *Fallschirmjäger* units on the new Eastern Front were going to have a lot to do. Throughout the winter, Major Walther Koch's *Sturmregiment*, although regularly isolated during Soviet attacks, was able to hold the vital airfield at Schaikowka (near Vitebsk) against all odds.

In the central sector, the MG Batallion fought at Yuchnov in support of the 4. SS Regiment and Flak units. A *Kampfgruppe* was formed under the command of General Major Eugen Meindl and the fighting would last until February 1942. Meindl would continue to lead this unit, serving with distinction, at the battles of Staraya Russa.

In the southern sector, FJR 2 was engaged along the River Mius while the 4. *Sturmregiment* was ordered to protect strategic roads. However, this was to prove very costly and during the winter of 1941-42 alone, losses among the *Fallschirmjäger* (the paratroopers who now become elite infantrymen), can be estimated at around 3,000 killed.

When spring returned, the majority of paratroop units were brought back to the Reich to reform and rebuild.

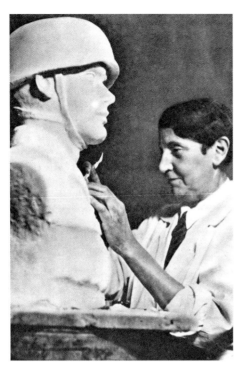

The famous German sculptor Milly Steger working on a bust of a *Fallschirmjäger*, probably an order for a cultural biennial.

The monument at Schaikowka Cemetery erected in honor of around 3,000 paratroopers who were killed during the winter of 1940-41. At least two recipients of the *Ritterkreuz* are buried here; *Leutnant* Helmut Arpke and *Oberfeldwebel* Heirnrich Orth. Arpke received his decoration for his participation in the capture of Eben Emael, while Orth was decorated posthumously for his good conduct in the East.

A combat group in the East. Their white outfits are clearly camouflaging well with the snow.

Log shelters were built to face the harsh winter.

A moment of rest in the warm. Note the white camouflage hanging from one of the walls.

Franz Bierl fought in Poland, serving in the *Heer*, as indicated by his uniform. He would later transfer to the paratroopers and was killed in the USSR, in early 1942.

Zum frommen Andenken im Gebete an

Franz Bierl,

Bauerssohn von Ulrichsgrün,
Unteroffizier, Fallschirmjäger,
Teilnehmer am Feldzug in Polen,

welcher am 6. Januar 1942 bei den
Kämpfen im Osten im Alter von 25
Jahren 5 Monaten den Heldentod für
das Vaterland fand.

Auf ferner, fremder Aue
Liegt er als toter Soldat.
Doch unvergessen ist er nicht,
Weil treu gekämpft er hat.
Und ist sein Grab auch ferne,
Vergessen wird er nicht.
Die Engelscharen werden
Ihn führ'n zum ew'gen Licht.
Zum Himmel ging er stille ein,
Mög leicht die Erde ihm nun sein!

**Er ruhe in Frieden.
Wir bitten seiner im Gebete
zu gedenken.**

Buchdruckerei G. A. Fuß, Waldmünchen.

When spring arrived, paratroopers returned their winter equipment to the quartermaster.

A moment of recollection at the grave of a comrade who has been killed in action.

Too often, the *Fallschirmjäger* were ordered to engage in anti-partisan missions.

The pleasure of returning to the country while the unit was being reorganised.

An anti-partisan mission returns in the USSR.

In heldenhaftem Einsatz fiel an der
Ostfront unser lieber, herzensguter
Sohn und Bruder

Alois Moser

Obergefreiter
bei einem Fallschirmjäger-Regiment
Inhaber des EK. I und II
sowie des goldenen
Fallschirmjägersprungabzeichens
geboren am 9. September 1921
in Lauingen
gefallen am 6. November 1942
im Osten
Seine Ruhestätte ist auf dem Heldenfriedhof des Regiments in Ribschewo

———

Wenn einer von uns müde wird,
Der and're für ihn wacht.
Wenn einer von uns zweifeln will,
Der and're gläubig lacht.
Wenn einer von uns fallen sollt,
Der and're steht für zwei,
Denn jedem Kämpfer gibt ein Gott
Den Kameraden bei.

Er starb für sein geliebtes Vaterland!

Alois Moser was killed
in action the USSR.
He was not deemed
to be a 'veteran' as he
was not reported to
have taken part in the
previous year's fighting
in Crete.

At the end of 1942, far from the sands of Africa, the snow returned to the USSR and the paratroopers fighting there put on their camouflage uniforms once more.

TTR (radio operators) in the USSR during the winter of 1942-43.

During the fighting for Velikiye Luki, paratroopers are seen taking shelter behind a *Sturmgeschütz* (assault cannon) III.

Chapter 2

Reinforcements and Various Projects

During these long months, Student and his staff had been meditating on the lessons learned from the Battle of Crete. However, they were still unaware of the existence of the Ultra decryption device that had thwarted the plans of Operation *Merkur*, almost turning the entire operation into a disaster for the invaders.

The most urgent need was to 'plug the holes' in the ranks and an important propaganda campaign was launched to encourage people to volunteer for the paratroopers. Many young Germans were easily convinced and, to accelerate training, in April 1942 the JRF 1, 3 and 4 were sent to France, particularly Normandy. Rotations took place, meaning the combat units were able to serve indirectly as occupation troops. One or two Normandy villages were also forcibly evacuated to allow the combatants to train for the infamous street fighting that had cost so many lives in Crete the previous year.

The II./FJR 1 took Mortain, then Vendome, in April 1942, fearing an attack by the British (which would actually take place in August, in Dieppe). In October 1942, assured of the region's stability, the high command recalled the regiment, which was stationed in Gardelegen. Student (and his officers) was eager to re-engage his paratroopers in significant combat as airborne troops, rather than just mere infantrymen. Various projects were planned: the airborne invasion of Malta (Operation *Hercules*) or the attack on Gibraltar (Operation *Felix*). Retrospectively, it is possible to think that if these operations had indeed taken place, the orders would have been intercepted by Ultra and the paratroopers would certainly have incurred losses equivalent, or superior, to those of Operation *Merkur*. The Germans even considered engaging airborne units in the Caucasus to force a passage through to the Baku oil fields. However, the next serious operation for the *Fallschirmjäger* (apart from the USSR) would take place in Africa.

To replace the losses suffered on Crete, new recruits arrived to fill the ranks of the paratroopers. Here, an officer inspects the newcomers.

Jump demonstrations in Berlin. An important propaganda campaign was launched to help recruit *Fallschirmjäger*, and here schoolchildren look on with admiration at the exhibition.

To support this call to arms, the Luftwaffe newspaper *Der Adler* increases the number of cartoons 'idealising' the paratroopers.

Above: Fallschirmjäger practice street fighting skills in a French village, which has been cleared of its inhabitants.

Opposite above: Young recruits learn to use the MG-34 machine gun.

Opposite below: An exercise drop in Normandy, 1942.

A platoon leader in Normandy.

Returning to barracks by truck after an exercise.

This accelerated training in France did not occur without 'breakages'. *Obergefreiter* Berliner Werner Dase was killed on 1 April 1944 during a particularly realistic exercise, and was buried with great pomp in the town of Vire.

The tomb of the unfortunate Dase. He now rests at the large German cemetery at La Cambe.

Above: In the west, training continues. This image shows a Pak (anti-tank) gun and its crew in the Netherlands.

Opposite above: *General* Kurt Student, accompanied by *Major i.G.* Arnold von Roon, arrives to inspect the recruits and is presented with a new type of parachute. *Major i.G.* von Roon had won his *Ritterkreuz* in Crete in May, 1941.

Opposite below: Newcomers to the *Fallschirmjäger* ranks.

During an exercise, a platoon leader gives the order to attack.

Replacements were needed throughout the war. In March 1944, *Gefreiter* Georg Fischl, a mechanic in II./JG 5, transferred to the paratroopers and, after a stay in Gardelegen, joined the *Fallschirmschule* (parachuting school) at Lyon-Bron. The *Fallschirmjäger* trainees now jumped from Ju 52 cabins laid on the ground.

If necessary, Fischl and his comrades were ordered to patrol the city of Lyon.

Chapter 3

Kampfgruppe Burckhardt and Fallschirm-Brigade Ramcke

At the end of 1941, British troops embarked on a counter-offensive in Libya, forcing the Italian-German units of *General* Erwin Rommel to retreat, and meaning that they needed reinforcements as soon as possible. A large detachment of the *Fallschirm-Lehr-Batallion* (primarily an anti-tank unit) was dispatched to Africa under the command of *Major* Walter Burckhardt. The 600 men travelled through Italy by train before crossing the Mediterranean by air. The adventure started badly after two soldiers were killed in a fire in Italy. On 7 January the men arrived at Castel Benito (Tripoli) and climbed aboard Italian trucks that would take them 500 kilometers away, to Wadi el Fara, on the new front.

Fighting took place, resulting in prisoners being taken and a number of *Fallschirmjäger* being killed. On 21 March 1942, *Kampfgruppe* Burckhardt regrouped at Derna airfield and would soon return to the Reich via Greece and Italy.

This engagement, which was largely improvised, was hardly a success. Although the soldiers had fought bravely, those paratroopers that had been sent to the desert in an emergency had had a hard time coping with Africa's climate. Diseases such as malaria, diarrhea etc. were common, and their limited food resulted in an unbalanced diet (hence a risk of scurvy and a general weakening of the body). They did not have enough equipment, and what they did have was not really adapted to the desert conditions.

This episode is relatively unknown in the history of the *Fallschirmjäger*, mainly because it was not exactly 'glorious'. Nevertheless, this 'test' would avoid a repetition of these 'failures' in future commitments in Africa.

Chapter 4

Fallschirm-Brigade Ramcke

While in France and Germany, the airborne units reformed with new recruits. At the same time, as the *Fallschirm*jäger units in the USSR continued fighting on the Eastern Front, the war in Africa was once more on a knife's edge by mid-1942. *Marshal* Rommel was able to capture Tobruk's fortress, but his *Panzerarmee Afrika* broke its teeth on the strong British defences near the Egyptian border. As a result, two new divisions and a parachute brigade were sent out, thus increasing the problem of supplying the Axis forces. *Luftwaffenjäger-Brigade 1* was formed and commanded by a very well-respected officer, *Generalmajor* Bernhard Ramcke, a veteran of the Battle of Crete. He was known as 'Papa' Ramcke as he had started his military career during the First World War in Belgian Flanders, serving with the *Marinekorps Flandern*.

The *Fallschirm-Brigade* Ramcke, as it would be more simply called afterwards, was made up of a set of detachments including anti-tank, artillery and pioneers. It would help combat the British troops, but the balance of power was changing every day and progressively benefited the opponent who, using its Egyptian bases, was able to receive reinforcements of men and equipment much more easily.

The Ramcke Brigade was shocked by the offensive launched by Marshal Bernard Montgomery on the evening of 23 October 1942, and consequently took part in the general retreat on 4 November, having suffered severe losses. Luckily, the *Fallschirmjäger* were able to capture a full British supply column and used the captured vehicles to return to their lines on 7 November. At the time of the regrouping in Fuka, there were only 600 left out of the 4,000 men who had been engaged in Africa. In spite of the transport difficulties and the harassment by the enemy, these soldiers were able to retreat to Tunisia in good order. This epic retreat, a kind of new Anabasis, meant that Ramcke was awarded the Oak Leaves to go alongside the Knight's Cross he had won in Crete in May 1941.

In Italy, a detachment from *Kampfgruppe* Burkhardt are seen embarking on a Ju 52 en route to Libya.

Burkhardt's men would soon discover the rigors of desert warfare.

A tracked motorcycle (Kettenkrad NSU) tows an Italian truck delivered to *Kampfgruppe* Burkhardt.

Rest in the desert. One of the unit's small recoilless guns can be seen in this image.

Paratroopers from *Kampfgruppe* Burkhardt who were killed in action were buried in the Libyan desert.

In mid-1942, a parachute brigade was sent to Africa under the orders of 'Papa' Ramcke. This *Kübelwagen* carries a letter 'R', the distinctive sign of this unit.

Marshal Rommel with *General* Ramcke.

A *Kettenkrad* tows a 37mm Flak gun.

Fallschirmjäger from Ramcke Brigade during the fighting at El Alamein.

Ramcke decorates his men after a battle.

Chapter 5

The Fallschirmjäger in Tunisia

Since 1941, the campaign in Africa had been a succession of back and forths along the coastal road. However, on 8 November 1942, the British landed in Oran and Algiers. The *Panzerarmee Afrika* was thus surrounded and needed to break out of the Tunisian enclave as soon as possible in order to maintain an Axis armed presence on the African continent.

Reinforcements were sent to Tunis, including airborne troops, which also meant those recalled from the Eastern Front, among others. Hard fighting took place around Bizerte in November between the *Fallschirmjäger* and the British vanguard. Faced with German obstinacy, the conflict very often turned into trench warfare, with soldiers digging trenches and foxholes to protect themselves. Attempts to land paratroopers and gliders behind British forces would also take place, but would mostly end in failure. (It seems that only commandos from the special 'Brandenburg' unit, the 'Reich commandos', would succeed in this type of operation).

At the beginning of 1943, the British Army pushed towards Tunis, but faced severe resistance from the FJR 5.

Each airborne unit would have its own story and adventure, often being called in as 'fire fighters' to counter an enemy offensive or launch raids on enemy lines. However, at the end of March 1943, the Mareth Defensive Line was broken and on 7 April, American forces joined the 8th British Army in El Hamma. The Tunisian pocket became a simple bridgehead, which gradually shrank smaller and smaller. Every day the Axis positions were nibbled away, with soldiers being killed on both sides, including many paratroopers.

On 9 May 1943, soldiers in the Tunis pocket were forced to surrender. The prisoners were divided between the victors and were sent into captivity in either Morocco, the USA or Canada.

In Tunisia, *Fallschirmjäger* are seen seeking cover under giant cacti to avoid being spotted by the ever-present Allied aircraft.

Zum frommen Gedenken

an den Kriegsfreiwilligen

LOTHAR BEIL

Obergefreiter

in einem Fallschirmjäger-Regiment

geboren am 28. Januar 1921

gefallen am 26. Februar 1943

in Tunesien (Afrika).

R. I. P.

The death card in memory of Lothar Beil, killed in Tunisia, makes it clear that this paratrooper was a former aviator, who was probably injured or 'knocked down' from his post. Many members of the flying corps would choose to enter the paratroop unit.

A quick meal taken between engagements on the front, in a well-camouflaged foxhole. The fighting in Tunisia would most often turn into positional warfare.

A *Fallschirmjäger* helps Tunisians to gather their crop. This was not just a propaganda photograph; the Tunisian population welcomed the Germans as brothers and liberators. This is because of Adolf Hitler's well-known opposition to the colonies and his alliance with the Grand Mufti of Jerusalem.

Leutnant Günther Frost in Tunisia. This officer, who was a member of the *Sturmregiment*, had joined his unit in the USSR before resting in France. During the Allied landing in Africa, he was urgently sent to Tunisia with his comrades.

Frost talking to British prisoners captured during a nightly raid on Allied lines.

The young paratrooper Gerhard Hoffmann, who was killed in Mateur.

Frommes Gebets-Andenken

an unseren lieben unvergeßlichen Sohn und Bruder

Gerhard Hofmann

Dentistensohn von Tittmoning
Fallschirmjäger bei einem
Afrikakorps

welcher am 10. April 1943 im Alter
von 23 Jahren den Heldentod gestor-
ben ist und in Mateur in Tunesien
begraben liegt.

Dein Grab im fernen Feindeslande
Ist uns wohl eine schwere Pein,
Doch nimm dies Wort zum Unterpfande:
„Dein Grab soll nicht verlassen sein!"
Allabends wenn die Glocken summen
Zieht liebend unser Geist dorthin,
Und streut dir betend Andachtblumen
Aufs Heldengrab mit frommem Sinn.

Druck von Anton Pustet, Tittmoning

Kriegsberichter (war correspondent) Batz was attached to the *Fallschirmjäger*, and here provides his vision of those paratroopers fighting in Tunisia.

Camels alongside a motorbike and sidecar.

The movement of troops always attracted the curiosity of the natives. But despite their sympathy for the Germans, Tunisia would soon be taken by the Allies.

Grave of paratrooper Wilhelm Paschall, probably in the large German cemetery in El Aouina (Tunis).

Chapter 6

Italy (1943)

After Tunisia had fallen, the German High Command were wary of an upcoming invasion of mainland Europe. But where would it be? In Greece? Or Sardinia? Against all expectations, it was to be Sicily, which although the most logical choice, was also the most predictable. With complete numerical superiority, the Allies launched Operation Husky in the early morning of 10 July 1943. Sicilian airfields were heavily bombed and the island was captured in a matter of days. To curb the Allied advance, the FJR 3, which at the time was stationed in the area around Avignon, was parachuted in south of Catania and supported detachments that were already stationed in Sicily (including *Kampfgruppe* Schmalz).

Heavy fighting took place once more, and again the *Fallschirmjäger* earned the respect of its opponent. But the waves of attack were impoosible to resist and, on 17 August, the last paratroopers left Sicilian soil at Messina and crossed the sea to the mainland. Allied optimism was cut short as the German retreat had been carried out perfectly. The British, who had thought they were attacking the German forces in a narrow area after being given detailed information by Ultra, were now at their enemy's expense. *Marshal* Albert Kesselring successfully evacuated a large number of units, which the Allied forces would later encounter on their slow progress north through mainland Italy.

However, the Sicilian campaign did claim one significant victim. Following the invasion of Italian territory and a heavy bombardment of Rome, *il Duce* Benito Mussolini was outvoted in the Fascist Grand Council. The king of Italy then had him arrested and the new Italian government, presided over by Marshal Pietro Badoglio, stated that he wished to continue the struggle alogside the Axis forces. Everyone knew, however, that in reality the king and Badoglio were preparing to change their allegiances. In the south of the country, the British begin to disembark and the German airborne units regrouped and rebuilt. Hitler then moved the 2nd division (2. FJD) from Avignon to the area surrounding Rome, on the pretext of strengthening the Wehrmacht on that side of the Alps. In fact, paratroopers were needed to secure the Italian capital during the approaching and predictable about-face of Badoglio.

On 8 September 1943, Italy announced it was pulling out of the war (which it hoped would take place soon, but it would in reality have to stay a little longer). Very soon, fighting took place in Rome and throughout Italy. If the 'Badoglio soldiers' were disarmed quickly, dozens of Italian paratroopers, who were opposed to their government's surrender, would join the ranks of the *Fallschirmjäger*. One of the most risky operations was conducted at the headquarters of the Italian Army at Monte Rotondo (north of Rome). This was not an improvised action, as the II./FJR 6 had been preparing for it in the south of Italy, in Foggia, since the fall of Mussolini. At 6:00 am on 9 September, Ju 52s loaded with paratroopers took off from Manfredonia aerodrome and headed towards their target. If a Ju 52 was fired upon, the *Fallschirmjäger* would jump out the aircraft and even if they were then scattered over the terrain, after a few hours they would ensure that they were masters of the whole area.

During this time, Hitler, who was always loyal in his friendships, was worried about the fate of the former *Duce*, and knew that Badoglio was ready to give him over to the Allies. German intelligence services investigated and the Führer sent his special envoy, *Hauptsturmführer* SS Otto Skorzeny, to Rome. On 12 September Operation Eiche was triggered. *Il Duce* was being kept on the Gran Sasso d'Italia, a mountain in the Abruzzo 2,914 m high. The only access to the hotel where he was being held was a cable car, but this was well-guarded by the Italians. There was reason to believe that in case of a traditional attack, the confronted guards would not kill their prisoner. The mountain summit therefore had to be reached by air, thus enjoying the element of surprise. However, the strong winds (at that height and over the mountain range) risked scattering any potential paratroopers. Consequently, the Germans returned to the good old DFS 230 glider, which had proved its worth at Eben Emael in 1940 and in Crete the following year. Ten were transported to Practica di Mare aerodrome and the operation was entrusted to *Oberleutnant* Georg Freiherr von Berlepsch. Afterwards, Skorzeny would claim all responsibility for himself, thus creating a myth which would be greatly amplified by propaganda and would even be continued after the war by a gullible media. Thanks to the skill and experience of their pilots, the gliders landed near the Hotel Campo Imperatore, despite the sudden and unpredictable air currents. The paratroopers ran out on all sides in order to neutralise the Italian soldiers, who were completely taken aback. Skorzeny presented himself to Mussolini and declared, '*Il Duce*, the *Führer* has ordered me to liberate you'. He proceeded to ride back with him in an Fi 156, which had come to collect the ex-prisoner, and proceeded to give himself all the credit for Operation *Eiche*, even though he was unable to plan such a delicate airborne operation himself, having never jumped with a parachute or piloted a glider before ... The paratroopers destroyed the enemy guns before descending into the valley. They made contact with their comrades who, under *Major* Harald Mors, in the meantime had encircled the Gran Sasso. The same night, Skorzeny would receive the *Ritterkreuz* and asked that it also be awarded to the pilot of his glider, *Leutnant* Elimar Meyer, of the LLG I. *Hauptman* Heinrich Gerlach, pilot of the Fi 156, also received the same high decoration, while Mors and von Berlepsch had to be content with the *Deutsche Kreuz im Gold* ...

Other operations took place throughout in Italy, such as the one bearing the code name *Goldfasan* (golden pheasant), on 17 September. Six hundred paratroopers from III./FJR 7 (commanded by *Major* Eduard Hübner) left Ciampino and were successfully dropped on the island of Elba. The Italian garrison capitulated soon after. After neutralizing Germany's former ally, most of the parachute units were sent south to support German troops who were defending the Reinhard and Gustav lines on the Volturno, near Monte Cassino. Meanwhile, 2.FJD, returned to the east to fight in Ukraine.

Paratroopers would now be fighting in Sicily and Italy.

An MG-42 position in southern Italy, 1943.

Staff discussion in Italy (General Bernhard Ramcke, centre).

Above: The burial of a paratrooper in a Provençal town.

Opposite above: *Fallschirmjäger* blowing up a bridge in the south of the country.

Opposite below: The 2. FJD had been sent to Provence in 1943 to be reformed. Young recruits are seen here recovering after a forced march near Avignon.

Above: The cushion decorated with medals carried during the funeral by a comrade proves beyond doubt that the deceased was a veteran.

Opposite above: After the fall of Mussolini, the 2. FJD would soon be victorious in Italy. Here, the division's commander, *Major* Harry Hermann, prepares for departure from the airfield at Avignon.

Opposite below: Another *Kriegsberichter* Batz drawing showing paratroopers destroying a railway bridge in Italy, in the face of the Allied advance.

Fallschirmjäger took control of Rome on 9 September. This image shows an unusual type of Pak gun.

In position at a crossroads in Rome, in front of the Castello Sant'Angelo.

Italian soldiers who were loyal to the Italian royal government were captured.

Progress is made through a pro-Badoglio city, under the protection of an assault gun.

DFS 230 gliders would be used to help free *il Duce*, who was being held on the Gran Sasso d'Italia. Here, paratroopers are training how to evacuate their aircraft as soon as possible.

Von Berlepsch's *Fallschirmjäger* prepare for Operation *Eiche*.

A dozen gliders are towed to the Gran Sasso by Ju 52s.

Thanks to the skill of their pilots, the DFS 230s landed near the Hotel Campo Imperatore, where *il Duce* was being guarded.

A cartoon from *Signal* magazine describing the blitz airborne attack.

After freeing *il Duce*, a radio is used to contact the authorities.

Mussolini and his liberators.

Paratroopers who had helped to clear the 'airstrip' watch the departure of Mussolini and Otto Skorzeny.

The final picture taken before the descent into the valley.

Les parachutistes qui se sont distingués lors de l'expédition du GranSasso, reçoivent la croix de chevalier des mains du Général des Aviateurs STUDENT

En reconnaissance de son héroisme dans la lutte pour l'avenir de notre peuple, le Führer a décoré le général d'aviation Kurt Student, comme 305ème soldat de l'Armée allemande, de la **FEUILLE DE CHÊNE DE LA CROIX DE CHEVALIER DE LA CROIX DE FER**

Le nom de ce général a été mentionné la dernière fois dans les communiqués relatant la libération du Duce. Ce sont en effet, des troupes de parachutistes, soumises à ses ordres, qui ont participé à cet acte d'éclat

Capitaine GERLACH

Sous-lieutenant MEYER

Operation *Eiche* would result in three *Ritterkreuz* being awarded to its participants: one for Skorzeny, one for the pilot of his glider and the third for the pilot of the Fi 156.

Discussions take place over a map.

Street fighting in an Italian city.

This 22-year-old *Gefreiter*, killed in Italy, had been promoted after his actions on Crete. However, he had clearly made several jumps, as evidenced by his badge.

Zum frommen Andenken
im Gebete an
Augustin Zißelsberger
von Deggendorf-Schaching
Gefreiter in einem Fallschirmjäger-Regt.
welcher am 28. Oktober 1943 in Italien im Alter von 22 Jahren 8 Monaten sein Leben für seine geliebte Heimat hingab.

Ehre seinem Andenken!

Buchdruckerei Seb. Weiß, Deggendorf.

Two big names from FJR 3; *Leutnant* Siegfried Rammelt and *Major* Rudolf Böhmler, in Italy. Rammelt would receive a posthumous *Ritterkreuz* after being killed in action on 21 March 1944, in the Cassino sector.

A telephone engineer in Italy.

Chapter 7

The Aegean Sea (1943)

The Italian surrender naturally influenced the situation in the Balkans, a region that was largely held by the Italian Army, as well as south-eastern Europe. In Rhodes, the Italian governor wanted to surrender and hand the sector over to the British forces. However, in a few hours, the German *Rhodos Sturmdivision* had soon taken control of the entire island. Of the entire archipelago, Rhodes had the only decent aerodromes, which certainly made it the capture of choice. Despite this serious setback, Winston Churchill persisted in wanting to capture the Dodecanese, an action that would allow him to counter the plans of his US-Soviet allies. He wanted to move via the Balkans to encircle the Wehrmacht forces who were engaged to the east. By an irony of history, the attack on Crete in May 1941 (Operation *Merkur*) was repeated: the Germans had control of the skies, the British of the seas. Fighting took place from island to island and, little by little, in October 1943, Kos, Patmos and other small islands that had been held by Italian forces were taken over (Operation *Eisbär*). For its part, the US military would do little for its independent 'ally', Britain. At the end of October, Leros, the 'Malta of the Aegean', was the last strong point held by the Italians and British in the Dodecanese. The island, bristling with guns, was formidable and any attack by sea would be extremely costly. The solution was a combined operation involving infantry soldiers of the *22 Infanteriedivision*, Brandenburg commandos (who were already fighting in Kos) and a detachment of paratroopers from I./FJR 2. At the beginning of November, about 400 *Fallschirmjäger* left Viterbo and were transported by Ju 52s to Tatoi (one of the aerodromes in Athens). On the morning of 12 November 1943, the attack on Leros began. The paratroopers jumped near Alinda Bay and, although warned of the plans by Ultra, the defenders could do little against this well-planned assault. The airborne troops quickly captured several batteries, thus allowing the landing of troops on the beaches. On 17 November, despite the regular supply of night supplies by the Navy, who had lost several buildings under the Stuka bombs, the Leros garrison was forced to surrender. This would be the last time in the Second World War that a complete British Army surrendered in open country.

For this brilliant action, the commander of the detachment, *Hauptman* Martin Kühne was awarded the *Ritterkreuz*.

The Italian surrender in September 1943 also affected Greece. *Gefreiter* Bernhard Buss (I./FJR 2) is about to jump on Leros, a strong point of the Dodecanese Islands.

Paratroopers jumping over Leros.

This was probably the last large-scale *Fallschirmjäger* drop of the Second World War.

Survivors regrop after the fall of Leros.

Hauptman Martin Kühne was awarded the Knight's Cross for capturing Leros. Despite his apparent youth, his decorations show that he destroyed five armoured vehicles and took part in dozens of close combats.

Chapter 8

Fighting in the East (1943-44)

By the end of 1943, the Red Army was continuing its progress and, far from jumping from Ju 52s or employing gliders as in Italy or Greece, the *Fallschirmjäger* continued to operate on this front as elite infantrymen. Their esprit de corps and speed of adaptation made them extremely formidable. The 2 FJD fought defensively at Shitomir and near Kirowograd alongside 11. Panzer Division. The fighting was particularly bloody during the resumption of fighting at Nowgorodka and the New Year took place under a deluge of fire from the famous 'Stalin's Organs' (rocket launchers).

In February, the division was engaged in attempts to break the encirclement of the Cherkassy pocket before retreating to the Dnjerst by April 1944.

The unit was temporarily withdrawn from the front to take on 600 reinforcements, who were then immediately re-engaged on the front with their comrades. This time, the fighting took place on the outskirts of Romania, very close to Moldova, which had been recaptured from the Soviets in 1941. East of Chisinau, between Dubossary and Butor, the *Fallschirmjäger* took part in a counteroffensive code named *Bollwerk*. They would be removed from the area in May 1944 to prepare for new engagements elsewhere. Several detachments, however, would be recalled in June to fight in Normandy.

The fighting in the USSR would, as usual, be very hotly contested.

Gedenket im Gebete

an unseren lieben, unvergeßl. Sohn u. Bruder

Lambert Schwarz

Mühl- und Sägewerks-Besitzerssohn
von Lengdorf

Obergefr. i. e. Fallschirmjäger-Reg.

Inh. des EK II und der Ostmedaille
Teilnehmer an den Kämpfen in Kreta,
bei Dieppe und Rußland
welcher bei den schweren Abwehrkämpfen
um Smolensk am 22. März 1943 durch Granat-
volltreffer bei Ablösung eines Sappenpostens
im 24. Lebensjahr den Heldentod für Gott und
Vaterland starb.
Er ruht im Heldenfriedhof Tinowka 75 km
nördlich Smolensk.

Die Pflicht rief mich zum Krieg hinaus,
Mit Gott ging ich vom Elternhaus,
Ich dachte Euer fort und fort,
Wenn ich auch weilt am fremden Ort,
Und freute mich auf's Wiederseh'n.
Wenn Krieg und Sturm zu Ende geh'n.
Doch anders hat's der Herr gewollt
Und hat von hier mich abgeholt.
Weiß nichts von Krieg und Erdenleid
Und bin von jeder Sorg befreit.
Drum tröstet liebste Eltern, Brüder u. Onkel
euch daran,
Was Gott tut, das ist wohlgetan.

Buchdruckerei R. Präbst, Dorfen

Lambert Schwarz

Lambert Schwarz was killed near Smolensk in 1943, and was already a veteran despite his young age. He had taken part in the Battle of Crete and his death card even specifies that he faced the Canadians during their raid on Dieppe on 19 August 1942, while his unit was stationed in France.

At the end of 1943, a large contingent of paratroopers left Italy and found themselves confronted with the vastness of the Russian Steppes, such as here in Kirowograd.

The *Fallschirmjäger* soon became acquainted with the rough living conditions in the USSR.

Major Hans Kroh (commanding I./FJR 2) observes the enemy lines through his binoculars, near a Pak (anti-tank) position. Kroh had received his Knight's Cross following the Battle of Crete. He would later add the Oak Leaves and the Swords and would then join the *Bundeswehr* after the war, where he achieved the rank of *Generalmajor*. He died on 18 July 1967.

On the Eastern Front, paratroop detachments continued the fight, often in cooperation with units from the *Heer*. They are seen here with a *Sturmgeschütz* (assault cannon) crew.

A quick meal in the East inbetween the fighting.

Heading to the Front at dusk.

Chapter 9

Italy (1944)

In early 1944, the Allies discovered that the re-capture of Italy was thwarted by the country's rugged terrain, which allowed the German defenders to use mountain ranges to construct strong lines of defence.

This was the case on the Volturno, with the Monte Cassino massif, which was the strong point of the famous Gustav Line. From the outset, the Germans had reported that the historic monastery built on the mountain would be free of occupation. For the ANZAC troops (Australian and New Zealand corps), this high-rise abbey appeared to 'taunt' the Allied soldiers. On 15 February 1944, the location will be heavily bombed by the Allies. The ruins, as they should be called, were immediately occupied by the *Fallschirmjäger*, who would set up an even more fierce resistance, earning themselves the nickname 'the Green Devils of Monte Cassino'.

German paratroopers not only blocked the Allied troops advancing from the south. Desperate to move north, the ambitious American general, Mark Clark, commander-in-chief in this theatre of war, launched Operation Anvil on 22 January 1944: a landing on the beaches of Anzio/Nettuno, south of Rome. This action had two advantages: bypass the Gustav Line and activate the capture of the Italian capital. However, they had not counted on *Marshal* Albert Kesselring's spirit, the *Oberbefehshaber Süd*, who sent all possible troops (including paratroopers) to this area in order to stop the invaders on the beaches.

However, the numerical superiority of the Allies was far too great and the Gustav Line was able to hold until 18 May before it was pushed back. The Battle of Monte Cassino cost the lives of 118,000 Allied soldiers and 20,000 Germans. British General Harold Alexander would pay tribute to the *Fallschirmjäger* by writing: 'Surely there is no troop of fighters in the world who could have stood up to such an ordeal and then gone on fighting with the ferocity they have'. In the process, to avoid being surrounded, Kesselring had to withdraw his men into positions around the bridgehead of Anzio and, on 5 June 1944, Rome (now declared an 'Open City' to avoid destruction) fell into Allied hands.

For almost a year, Allied troops would continue their slow progress north, finally reaching the Alps in May 1945. Many paratroopers of the 1. and 4. FJD would participate in the fighting that took place during this time, and would fall on Italian soil.

At the end of 1943, the snow surprised many of the soldiers, who had imagined fighting in a country '*wo die Zitronen blühen*' ('where lemons grow').

A lookout station on a snowy mountain in Italy.

Marshal Albert Kesselring (always smiling) and *Generalleutnant* Richard Heidrich visited the front following the Allied landings at Anzio/Nettuno. Heidrich died in a British camp in December 1947.

Paratroopers at Anzio.

An improvised shelter near Anzio.

Mail and packages are handed out.

Taking a break in Anzio. These *Fallschirmjäger* are seen at a farm, under the watchful eye of the owners; a couple of Italian peasants, who were unwilling to desert their property despite the proximity of the front.

A paratrooper at Nettuno. This photograph, taken from *Der Adler* magazine, highlights the extreme youth of many of the fighters.

In the ruins of the abbey at Monte Cassino.

Positioned in the ruins of the destroyed abbey, these paratroopers have set up mortars in what was once a courtyard.

Having just descended from Cassino, these exhausted fighters are warmly welcomed by their comrades.

A detachment of the 'Cassino Green Devils' is greeted at Air Marshal Hermann Göring's headquarters.

Gebetsandenken

an unsern innigstgeliebten Sohn u. Bruder

Josef Bergermeier

von Malmersdorf

Uffz. in einem Fallschirmjäger-Rgt.

welcher am 4. März 1944 bei den schweren Kämpfen um Cassino im Alter von
22 Jahren den Heldentod starb.

Wir warteten und hofften immer
Doch Du kehrst nimmermehr zurück.
Verblaßt ist nun der Hoffnung Schimmer
Und tränenfeucht ist unser Blick.
Es irrt das Aug' in weite Fernen
Sucht Deines Sterbens heiligen Ort
Und ruft zum Lenker aller Schlachten
Zu Dir, o Vater, ein flehend Wort:
O führe diesen toten Krieger
In Deine Herrlichkeiten ein.
Er gab sein Leben für die Brüder
Laß es vor Dir ein Opfer sein!

Vater unser · Ave Maria

J. Kral & Co., Abensberg

A young combatant killed in Cassino.

US Army MPs gather prisoners at Anzio before evacuating them by boat. One of the prisoners is a paratrooper and can be identified by his camouflage jumpsuit.

New recruits continued to expand the ranks of the *Fallschirmjäger* in 1944. Some of them were young men, others were older soldiers transferred from their original units. All, however, were volunteers and would continue to make jumps even if airborne operations were relatively rare on the front. Here, parachutes are being inspected before a jump.

In 1944, the Wehrmacht's misery was blatant, but paratroopers were still forced carry out practice jumps using He 111s. The Ju 52 trimotors, which by this time were quite rare, were scattered on all fronts.

Sometimes old Heinkel 111s were put back into service.

Savoia transport planes, which had been taken from the former Italian Air Force, were also used.

A *Kettenkrad* and trailer on the Anzio Front.

Anzio/Nettuno.
A paratrooper unit
gains new positions.

Gott, der Herr, rief in die Heimat des
ewigen Friedens aus dem Kampffeld in
Italien den

Gefreiten in einem Fallschirmjäger-Regmt.

Johann Labmayer

Bauernsohn in Niederham, Pfarre
St. Marienkirchen

welcher am 5. Februar 1944 bei
Nettuno für Führer, Volk und
Vaterland im 20. Lebensjahre den
Heldentod starb.

Eltern, Geschwister und Freunde mein,
So gern schrieb ich aus der Ferne heim,
Doch heute ist es zum letzten Mal,
Daß ich Euch grüße tausendmal.
Und sage Dank für jede Gab,
Die ich von Euch empfangen hab,
Richte an Euch die letzte Bitt',
Vergeßt ja im Gebet mich nicht.
Nur keine Träne, keine Klag,
Der liebe Gott, der mir das Leben gab
Rief mich so früh ins Heldengrab.

Zweigniederl. Bruckmayr, St.Marienkirchen

Pflichterfüllung bis zu Letzten,
dies war der Sinn Deines Lebens

Killed south of Rome,
aged 20.

Action in a courtyard of what was once the abbey of Monte Cassino.

Two *Fallschirmjäger* in the debris of the abbey. The Gustav Line would soon be pushed back.

Rome, early June 1944. *Gefreiter* Bernhard Buss and his comrades drop down into a sewer, which provides a natural shelter from the Allied fighter bombers that dominated the air. Buss is seen here examining the sky with some trepidation.

Rome, an open city. With the Colosseum in the background, this German sidecar is seen evacuating the Eternal City.

Rome, 5 June 1944. These four captured paratroopers being interrogated by GIs in the Piazza Esedra (now the Piazza della Repubblica).

Chapter 10

The Normandy Invasion (1944)

At this time, the paratroop units lacked soldiers and any reinforcements were most welcome. However, little by little, the high command began to reduce the number of air units, even down to entire squadrons. Just like the wounded paratroopers who were declared unfit to jump, the number of mechanics, parachute repairers, cooks, etc. would be offered a somewhat limited choice: to be poured into the land forces, either the *Waffen-SS*, *Fallschirmjäger*, or *Flak*. Thus, as early as 1944, older men (but still with some combat experience) expanded the ranks of the airborne.

Now was the time! On 6 June 1944, the Allies landed in Normandy (Operation Overlord), in an event that would eclipse the successful German capture of Rome the day before.

Following a reorganistation of the paratroop units, in April 1944 *II. Fallschirmkorps* had been sent to Brittany, under the orders of *General* Meindl. From 7 June, detachments from the corps would be sent to Normandy, where fierce fighting was taking place, allowing the *Fallschirmjäger* to show their ability to lead a guerrilla warfare, taking advantage of the many hedges that streaked across the Normandy landscape. Those who particularly distinguished themselves were the men of 6.FJR, commanded by *Oberst* August von der der Heydte, a veteran of the Battle of Crete, who would earn the nickname, 'the Lions of Carentan'.

On 1 August 1944, *Generalleutnant* Ramcke was named *Festungskommandant* of Brest. He recieved orders for the men of 2. FJD to hold the port, called 'Fortress' (*Festung*), for as long as possible and to prevent it from falling into enemy hands. The port remained in German hands until 19 September 1944 and it has been estimated that the siege detained 50,000 GIs, who would otherwise have been more useful elsewhere. Other *Fallschirmjäger* would take part in the defence of St Nazaire, which would hold until May 1945.

Paratroop units, often scattered by the fighting, would take part in all actions during the retreat, and many of these men would be captured or killed on the road to the Reich. During the great battle around Mons (near the border between France and Belgium) at the beginning of September, whole units were destroyed. However, some groups of airborne troops succeeded, often with difficulty, to escape the American forces, as well as the Resistance, and cross the German border at night to reinforce the defense of the Westwall.

During this retreat, many local dramas took place when brave civilians, 25th-hour resisters armed with odds and ends, wanted to play the 'hero' by intercepting the soldiers, who asked for only one thing: that they were left free to travel back to the east. Such confrontations between the 'highly-trained and battle-hardened men' and pitiful civilians would regularly turn to the advantage of the latter, whose names would soon be seen written on the war memorials in their towns and villages.

On the day Rome fell, *Gefreiter* Fischl was ordered to guard the Morlaix Bridge (Brittany) with an MG-42. The next day (6 June), an important and decisive landing would take place in Normandy.

In Brittany, the *Fallschirmjäger* had multiplied their activities.

Combined exercises also took place with the *Heer*. In this image, *Major* Harry Hermann is seen with the tank general, Leo Geyr von Schweppenburg.

General Eugen Meindl comes to encourage his men as they leave for the new Normandy Front.

A paratrooper ready to ambush the Allies in Normandy with an FG-42.

Gott der Herr rief in die Heimat des ewigen Friedens aus dem Kampffeld im Westen den

Gefreiten in einem Fallschirmjäger-Rgmt.

Hermann Bauer

aus Hackenbuch, Pfarre
St. Marienkirchen

welcher am 15. Juni 1944 bei einem feindlichen Gegenstoß im Raume St. Lo (Frankreich) im 19. Lebensjahre den Heldentod für Volk und Heimat fand.

Liebe Mutter und Geschwister mein,
Ich kehre nicht mehr zu Euch heim,
Der letzte Gedanke, letzte Blick,
Der eilte noch zu Euch zurück.
Als ich starb im Feindesland,
Reichte niemand mir die Hand.
Doch eh' mein Auge war gebrochen,
Sah ich schon den Himmel offen.

In Gottes Ratschluß steht geschrieben
Es seh'n sich wieder, die sich lieben.

Zweigniederl. Bruckmayr, St. Marienkirchen

PBD 56

Killed aged 19 years old in St-Lô, this paratrooper had not experienced the *Fallschirmjäger*'s earlier campaigns.

The motorcyclist in this *Feldgendarmerie* detachment is a lot older, and is therefore probably a 'veteran' who has recently been drafted into the paratroopers.

The *Feldgendarmerie* were disliked by the troops due to their rigorous actions. They were given the derogatory nickname '*Kettenhunde*' (Chain-dogs) after the gorgets they wore around their necks.

Leutnant Joachim Meissner was killed in St Jean-de-Daye on 25 July 1944. He had 'won' his *Ritterkreuz* at Eben Emael in May 1940, having served as part of the 'Eisen' detachment under Koch.

A *Sanitäter* (medic) in his foxhole in Normandy.

Meindl comes to thank and decorate the combatants.

A *Panzerschreck* was the equivalent of the American bazooka.

A well-camouflaged mortar crew.

Oskar Maurer

Feldwebel und Komp.-Truppführer in einem Fallschirmjäger-Regiment, Inhaber versch. Auszeich-
nungen, Teilnehmer an den Feldzügen auf Kreta,
in Griechenland, im Osten, in Italien und in der
Normandie, gefallen am 6. 7. 44 im Westen im
Alter von 25 Jahren.

Oskar Maurer was killed in Normandy on 6 July
1944. He was a veteran of both the Crete and
Italian campaigns.

Exchanging weapons
in-between the fighting.

A local headquarters.

In nie erlöschender Liebe u. zum steten Gedenken an unseren tapferen Sohn und Bruder

Georg Brüderl

Obergefr. in einer Fallschirm= Abteilung
welcher am 20. August 1944 im Alter v. 24 Jahren nach 6 ½ jhr. Dienstzeit in Frankreich sein Leben für seine geliebte Heimat opferte.

A. Miller & Sohn, Traunstein

Given his age and rank, *Obergefreiter* Brüderl was clearly a 'veteran' aviator and perhaps formally a bomber gunner whose unit had been disbanded.

Ehre feinem Andenken!

———

Er gab alles, fein Leben, fein Blut,
Er gab es hin mit heiligem Mut.
Er opferte Zukunft und Jugendglück,
Er kehrt nie mehr zur Heimat zurück.

✝

Gedenket in Liebe und ſtiller Trauer des
tapferen Soldaten

Karl Hartl

Gefreiter in einem Fallſchirmjäger-Regt.,
kaufm. Angeſtellter,
Landwirtsſohn von Reichersdorf,

welcher im Auguſt 1944 im Alter von 21
Jahren nach ſchwerer Verwundung in Breſt
(Frankreich) verſtorben iſt.

O braver Sohn und Bruder, haſt beendet
In heißer Schlacht Dein junges Leben Du,
Auf Feindesboden ſchwer und müde
Sank hin Dein Haupt zur letzten Ruh.
Nun ruhe ſanft, Du gutes, braves Herz
Wer dich gekannt, fühlt unſern Schmerz.

Druck: Wegmann, Landau-Iſar

Above: Ramcke was ordered to defend '*Festung* Brest'. The battle would cause many casualties on both sides.

Opposite above: These wounded were lucky. They were evacuated from Normandy to Paris and are seen en route to a hospital in the Reich.

Opposite below: 'Papa' Ramcke talks with young paratroopers (note his 'Afrika' armband). As an officer, Ramcke was greatly appreciated by his subordinates.

Above: As the paratroopers retreated to Germany, one of them has been taken prisoner in Chartres by civilians. It is unknown whether or not he survived for long, as many such prisoners were executed by pseudo-resistants.

Opposite above: Ramcke, his dog, and the garrison of Brest were forced to surrender on 19 September 1944.

Opposite below: Now prisoners of war, the defenders of Brest are assembled together. Soldiers from the *Heer* are stood next to the *Fallschirmjäger*.

Chapter 11

The Netherlands and the Ardennes

The German retreat had stopped at the border of the Reich and the Netherlands, where defensive lines could be established against Allied armies, whose supply lines were beginning to be severely stretched. Once again, Britain wanted to go it alone, and Montgomery somewhat imprudently launched the famous Operation Market Garden; a massive airborne operation on the Dutch sector around Arnhem. Trusting the information from Ultra, the British marshal thought the area would be free from enemy units. However, shortly before the operation began, two SS divisions had gathered in this area to regroup and the British airborne found themselves fighting not only unexpected enemies, but also *Fallschirmjäger* detachments who had assembled as reinforcemnts. From Arnhem to the Dutch-Belgian border, other airborne units (often fighting as part of a *Kampfgruppe*) slowed the advance of the ground troops who were pushing towards Arnhem, and assisted in the collapse of this airborne operation, which had been too ambitious and dogged by fate. The German paratroopers would manage to hold on to the region until almost the end of 1944, giving their opponents a rough ride in the process.

In December 1944, the Allies rested on their laurels. For them, the defeat of the Reich was only a matter of weeks away and, as Ultra failed to announce any significant troop movements, the die seemed cast. Allied intelligence had become numb by relying on one source only. The Germans had begun to understand that their plans were being foiled and, for the planned surprise offensive code named *Wacht am Rhein*, Enigma was used sparingly.

On 16 December 1944, the German attack launched in the Ardennes surprised the Allies at first. At dawn, Operation *Stösser* began: some 850 paratroopers were dropped north of Malmedy, in the American rear. However, the Luftwaffe was no longer able to fulfill its ambitions, and *Stösser* ran out of steam. Ju 52s flew off course in the darkness, others were shot down by the Allied DCA, and some come back prematurely. Only 100 men managed to reach their designated target, but this was not enough to constitute a fighting force. Tracked down by the GIs, the paratroopers, including their commander, *Oberst* von der Heydte, were captured - often in a very bad state. The last major use of German paratroopers during the Second World War was therefore a total failure.

On the ground, paratroop units were now used as infantrymen. However, given the declining quality of recruits (men who were either too old or too inexperienced), these soldiers should not have been expected to work miracles, and would consequently suffer heavy losses around Bastogne and the rest of the Ardennes (including the Grand Duchy).

In January 1945, the Battle of the Bulge was inexorably lost for the Reich.

Many *Fallschirmjäger* were captured during the great battle around Mons at the beginning of September 1944, such as these seen here, who are being interviewed by GIs at Hyon.

These paratroopers were captured by partisans in the Walcourt (Namur) region as they walked towards the German border. They appear to have been treated well and are seen posing with their 'jailers'.

During their advance towards the end of 1944, the Allies commandeered various barracks that had been occupied shortly beforehand by their opponents. In Metz, a hospital was set up in a building that contained a giant mural to the glory of German paratroopers.

Despite the collapse, German forces were able to retreat to defensive lines in the Netherlands and at the Reich's borders. In September, a Canadian tank commander captured a paratrooper in the city of Sint-Michielsgestel near Tilburg. The prisoner is not a youngster and must therefore be a 'veteran' who had been recently posted to an airborne unit.

By keeping the Allies away from Arnhem, German paratroopers contributed greatly to the failure of the Allied airborne operation there (Operation Market Garden).

In Gottes hl. Frieden ruht fern
von seinen Lieben unser lieber Sohn
und jüngster Bruder

Leander Brucklachner,

Fallschirmjäger,

geb. am 19. 8. 1926 in Bonsal,
gest. infolge schwerer Verwundung
am 16. 11. 1944 am Hauptverbands-
platz in Rotterdam (Holland).

Gefallen! Diese Schreckenskunde,
schlug in unsern Herzen tiefe Wunden
er, der so lieb war und so gut,
hingeben mußte er sein teures Blut.
Du hast uns ja so oft geschrieben,
macht keine Sorgen euch Ihr Lieben,
ich kehr zurück, auf Wiedersehn.
Doch kann es jetzt nicht mehr geschehn.
Und sollten einst die Friedensglocken klingen,
die Sieger jubelnd in die Heimat ziehn,
dann werden heißer unsere Tränen fließen
und traurig werden wir zur Seite stehn.

Mein Jesus Barmherzigkeit.

Vater unser.

Buchdruckerei A. Schloegel, Vöttmes

Wer Dich gekannt, der liebte Dich,
Wer Dich geliebt, vergißt Dich nicht.

This young paratrooper died in a military hospital in Rotterdam, not long after his eighteenth birthday.

In December 1944, Operation *Wacht am Rhein* (the Battle of the Bulge) began in the Ardennes. The Allies were initially surprised, which resulted in local success, such as for these *Fallschirmjäger*, seen here being transported on a *Königstiger*.

Operation *Wacht am Rhein* should have been preceded by Operation *Stösser*, a large paratroop drop on the American rear. However, the 1944 pilots no longer had the same skills as their predecessors, and the operation would be a catastrophe. In this image, GIs examine the wreck of a Ju 52 that has been shot down by the DCA, surrounded by corpses of paratroopers.

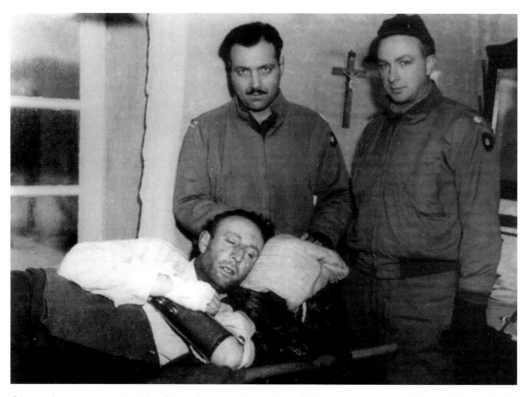

Oberst August von der Heydte, who led Operation *Stösser*, was captured by soldiers of the 99th US Infantry Division in a state of exhaustion and hypothermia on 22 December. There was consequently no glory to the end of the war for this Battle of Crete veteran.

In spite of their efforts, this time the paratroopers were unable to push the Allies back to the sea.

Improvised grave of a German paratrooper in the woods near Bastogne.

Zum frommen Andenken
an unsern lieben Sohn und Bruder

Rudolf Manetsberger

gefallen 26. Dezember 1944 in Luxemburg im Alter von 17¹/₂ Jahren.

Fürs Vaterland in schwerster Stunde
Gab ich mein junges Leben hin.
Wohl schrecklich war für euch die Kunde,
Daß nun auch ich gefallen bin.
Ich ruhe meinem Bruder gleich
Vom Kampf nun aus in fremder Erde
Und hoffe, daß im Himmelreich
Ein Wiederseh'n uns allen werde.

Gebr. Geiselberger, Altötting

Paratrooper Manetsberger was killed in Luxemburg aged 17 and a half.

Chapter 12

'Until the Bitter End'

From January to May 1945, the remnants of the paratroop units would fight fiercely and resolutely on all fronts: in Italy, in the East, or in various *Kessels* (cauldrons) in the West. This part of their story remains relatively unknown. So, as one Berlin paratrooper remembered: 'In April 1945 we received parachutes ready for the jump. Usually, we prepared the parachutes ourseleves. This type of parachute implied a special mission and, indeed, we boarded a plane in order to be dropped near a bridge on the enemy's rear. We blew it up.' These small comando operations did not have to be exceptional, but were always led by a small group of determined men. To date, nobody has been able to draw up a list of who was involved, and these brilliant actions will sink into oblivion.

On 8 May 1945, the Second World War ended in Europe and, whether in Germany or Italy, the surviving paratroopers would be captured in their thousands.

In the East, serious fighting took place in Lithuania. Here, paratroopers are advancing behind a Tiger tank.

Fallschirmjägers advance while being protected by a Tiger.

Lithuania. These paratroopers are heading to the Front with a calf, probably to try and improve the mundaneness of their ordinary days.

Gefreiter Buss takes a short rest in Florence, Italy. He will soon return to the fighting that would not end until May 1945.

This paratrooper, who was captured at Weymertz, also appears to be very young, even though he is trying to hide his face. However, he is wearing the parachute jump badge, a *Hitlerjugend* badge, and also that of the EK II (whose ribbon is visible).

This other *Fallschirmjäger*, who is just as young, is obviously much happier to have been captured by American troops.

A column of prisoners (including several paratroopers) near Bastogne.

Three *Fallschirmjäger* at the end of the war. One of them sports the armband worn by Battle of Crete veterans.

Fatigue can be read on the faces of these men, who nevertheless, would fight to the end.

Fighting in the East would continue to be very bloody until 8 May 1945.

Zum frommen Andenken im Gebete
an
Hans Glindemann
Zeichner
Uffz. in einer Fallschirmtruppenabtlg.
Inh. des E.K. 1 und 2
Gefallen am 5. Februar 1945
im Osten im 28. Lebensjahre.

Du warst so jung, Du warst so gut,
für's Vaterland gabst Du Dein Blut.
Dein stilles Herz ruht nun in Frieden
Ewig beweint von Deinen Lieben

Vater unser!   Ave Maria!

Druck: Frz. Wohlwend, Schierling

Orders probably being given during the fighting in one of the many *Kessel* (cauldrons) in the West.

The *Fallschirmjäger* would lose several of their numbers in Alsace.

Den Heldentod starb unser lieber Sohn
und guter Bruder, Schwager

Joh. Bapt. Pfeffer

Bauerssohn von **Hölzelsried**

Uffz. einer Fallschirm-Jäger-Regt.

gefallen am 19. Januar 1945 im Elsass
im Alter von 28 Jahren.

Gar weit von meiner Heimat mußt ich sterben
Des Feindes Kugel brachte mir den Tod
Ich fiel in Mitte meiner Kameraden
Und zog mit diesen heim zum lieben Gott
Die Sternlein weihn mir ihren hl. Schimmer
Und grüßen meines Grabes stillen Ort.
O seid getrost, es leuchtet mir für immer
Das ewige Licht in meiner Heimat dort!

Druck: Anton Lackerbauer, Regen, Tel. 78

Fighting in a ruined factory in the Reich, whose territory was shrinking by the day ... On the Western Front, fighting often took place in *Kessels*; small pockets of German resistance surrounded by Allied forces.

Exhausted, this section chief takes a little rest on the ground.

Seine Heimatliebe besiegelte mit dem
Heldentode unser lieber unvergessener
Sohn und Bruder

Karl Meier

Bauerssohn von Mossendorf
Obergefreiter in einem Fallschirmjäg.-Rgt.

geboren am 2. Juni 1921
gefallen am 1. Februar 1944

Tausend Dank sei dem von Herzen
Der im Grab an mich noch denkt
Und aus seinem guten Herzen
Mir ein Vater unser schenkt.

Mein Jesus, Barmherzigkeit.
Vater unser. — Ave Maria

Seine Heimatliebe besiegelte mit dem
Heldentode unser lieber unvergessener
Sohn und Bruder

Georg Meier

Bauerssohn von Mossendorf
Gefr. i. e. Fallschirm-Pionier-Sturmbatl.

geboren am 24. Januar 1926
gefallen am 29. März 1945 bei Braakfost in Holland
Er folgte seinem Bruder Karl nach einem Jahr und
zwei Monaten im Heldentode nach

Du sankst dahin wie Rosen sinken
Wenn sie in voller Blüte stehn.
Und heiße bittere Tränen fließen
Bis wir uns einstens wiedersehn.

Vater unser. — Ave Maria.

GEORG BRAND BUCHDRUCKEREI REGENSBURG

Two paratrooper brothers. Karl was killed in February 1944, while Georg would suffer the same fate in March 1945.

A Tiger tank brings back its load of exhausted paratroopers in East Prussia. The Wehrmacht's surrender is near...